More
ROLF HARTUNG **Creative Textile Design**

COLOR AND TEXTURE

 NEW YORK **Reinhold Publishing Corporation**

126939

CONTENTS

Illustrations are of work by the author and his pupils, except:

Figs 6, 7 and 8 (G. Hein); 52 and 53 (H. Seifert); 5, 68, 69 and 138 (K. Rhotert); and 42 and 57 (H. Wredow).

In illustrations, B denotes boys and G girls; these symbols are followed by the age of the child.

TEXTURE

The making of textiles is conditioned by the fact that cloth can be woven of any desired length but only of limited width. As its threads lie at right angles to each other, this restricts uncut cloth to rectangular shapes but also permits warp and weft to be separated without cutting. Handkerchiefs, head-scarves and neckerchiefs are typical of square pieces of cloth. Oblong pieces are blankets, curtains, towels and mats; scarves and ribbons are very narrow oblongs. The nature of any work with textiles depends to a great degree on which of these three basic shapes, varying from the regular-sided plane via the rectangle to the linear strip, are chosen.

Cloth to be dyed should have warp and weft of equal tension and good absorption capacity. Linen and above all cotton are the most suitable materials. Cloth that has been dressed with preparations containing fats or starch, which cover the threads unequally, should have them removed by washing with hot water and soap, and rinsing. The material is then ready for the various processes after a light ironing.

Frequently a second and very light application of starch may be made. This allows any unevenness to be smoothed down (10) or a delicate pattern to be applied (139); it can prevent the dye from penetrating too quickly (2,7,8) or wax from adhering too firmly. For this purpose the best starch is a mixture of rice flour and water (one spoonful of rice flour per square yard). This kind of starch spreads evenly through the material and can easily be removed subsequently with warm water.

For all methods of dyeing, except by folding or binding, the material should be stretched tightly over wooden frames with all threads kept straight. The minimum size of frame is $8\frac{1}{4}''$ by $8\frac{1}{4}''$, the maximum 2' by 2'8''; the wood should be $1\frac{1}{2}''$ wide by $\frac{1}{2}''$ deep. For larger dimensions the surplus material can either be re-stretched or—which is more difficult—gradually unrolled from a spindle, one hand keeping the material tightly stretched while the other hand applies the pattern. Before dyeing, the prepared cloth must be 'loosened' by damping it; after dyeing it should be rinsed in water, smoothed out on a flat surface and dried or ironed.

COLOUR

Only liquid dyes penetrate lastingly into the fibres of cloth. Paste dyes, used in fabric printing, cannot amalgamate so thoroughly with the material, and therefore the processes described in this book are restricted to those using liquid dyes, in particular water-soluble dyestuffs which are usable in a cold or lukewarm solution.

Fast, compatible textile dyestuffs are generally obtainable at retail shops in small packages sufficient to dye material of up to half a pound in weight. The powder dye is dissolved in boiling water and passed through a sieve in order to collect any small solid lumps of dye. The concentrated dye is then thinned with lukewarm water to the required dilution. To increase the adhesion of the dye, one dessert-spoonful of cooking salt per 3 oz. weight of cloth is added. The resulting solution is known as the 'dye-bath'. Since dyed material often dries considerably paler than it looks while the dye is still wet, it is advisable to dye trial strips and dry them. With the aid of these trials the ratio of dye to water can be altered to reach the required colour. It should be noted that the results obtained from a dye-bath are more durable than from cold-water dye. A weaker solution over a long time dyes more intensively than a strong solution over a short time.

The solution in the dye-bath can be kept for weeks. Tall-sided oblong plastic vessels are better suited for making and keeping dye-baths than round bowls, since rectangular lengths of cloth are more easily dipped into a container of this shape. Metal containers should be avoided, as they may oxidise and affect the dye and are more difficult to clean.

It should be noted that there are two distinct ways of dyeing:

1. Dyeing onto the material

2. Dyeing into the material.

In the first process the dye is applied by dabbing, painting or stippling, by pouring or by rapid immersion of the fabric. The blobs of colour spread, their shape depending on the method used.

The nature and quality of the dye should be kept under constant scrutiny: its intensity of tone and colour depends directly on the thickness of the solution. Gradations, mixtures of colours and the juxtaposition of two or more pure colours can also be achieved (see Plate IV opp. p. 64).

The dyes can be put into small containers, as they are only required in small quantities. The educative value of dyeing lies in the freshness, immediacy and simplicity of the results: against this must be set the likelihood of the colours fading fairly rapidly.

In the second process, after 'masking'—a method of preventing certain areas of the fabric from receiving the dye—the fabric is completely immersed in the dye-bath. (Time of immersion: 15-30 minutes.) The material should be completely covered by the dye and kept in continual movement. While the fabric is soaking the degree of colouration cannot be accurately judged. It can be checked from time to time by taking the fabric out of the solution and allowing surplus dye to drain off. The advantage of this method lies in the ability to achieve the uniform dyeing of large pieces of cloth in a single process. It is used when masking with wax or by the binding method.

The characteristics of the techniques of 'masking' are best shown when a strong contrast of light and dark between the masked area and the dyed area is achieved. Examples of this are shown in the book with specimens of contrast between white and venetian red.

Monochrome dyeing with partial masking of a white fabric demands care, precision and a thorough knowledge of methods and materials. This process should always be mastered before proceeding to polychrome dyeing. If yellow fabric is masked instead of white, a further cold and warm contrast is added to that of light and dark if blue dye is used, whilst a red dye reduces the force of contrast as red and yellow are closely related colours. This, of course, is still achieved with only a single dyeing process.

If a fabric is to receive more than one colouring it can be done in two ways:

After masking, the fabric is dipped and dyed several times in succession and all masking is removed simultaneously at the end of the sequence, leaving all the unmasked areas dyed with a single colour which has been deepened in tone with each successive immersion. This method can only be used when dying from a light to a darker colour, since light-toned textile dyes are ineffective on a ground of a darker colour. (Plate I, opp. p. 16, shows series dyeing with double masking by binding; Plate II, opp. p. 32, a similar process with candlewax masking.)

The second method is to remove the masking after each immersion, re-mask the fabric and then dye the areas previously kept clear. The greater creative freedom offered by this method also involves more work. It is only worth using if the main object is a polychrome effect and colour overlap is unimportant. Colours may be applied in any sequence (see Plate III, opp. p. 48—dyeing in sequence with candlewax lines).

Both these techniques consist of a succession of like processes, in which the foregoing ones determine those to follow. Since the work takes a relatively long time it demands a degree of stamina.

In Indonesia these techniques, known as 'Batik', are still used. Batik is not an artistic museum-piece. It is a living craft, the skill being passed on from hand to hand. Traditional patterns are continually being modified and enriched with endless variations, an example of a genuine and vigorous folk-art kept alive by an education which is predominantly aesthetic in content.

Unlike Batik, which relies on traditional patterns, the creative play described in this book has no such ties and draws its rules only from the inherent limitations imposed by the materials.

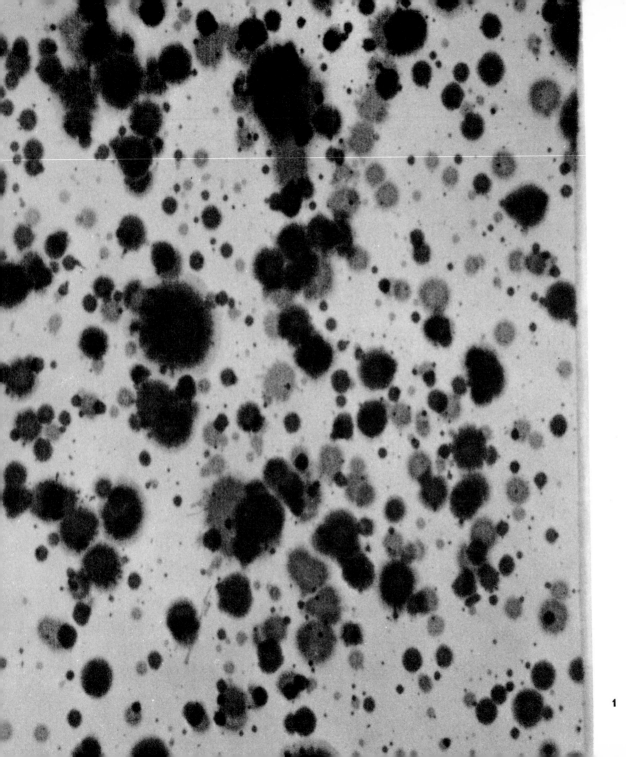

1

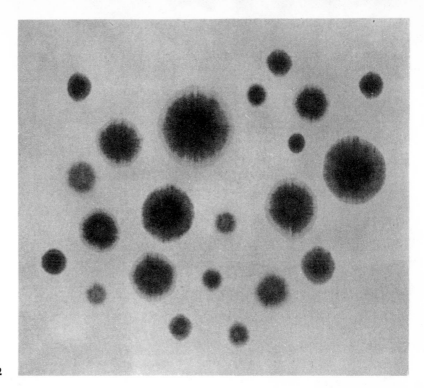

2

Dye sprayed on to fabric. The blobs of dye spread out in circles on the horizontally stretched cloth. Bright yellow dye is partially covered by superimposed blobs of the darker red (1).

When no forces are acting on it, any quantity of fluid will always tend to form a sphere. If this sphere encounters a material of even texture it will, under most conditions, spread out in a circular plane: hence the round blobs formed by drops of dye on fabric. The density of colour lessens from the centre outwards, as the diffusion of the fluid carries the particles of dye for distances which vary according to their size (2). The outermost rings of the circles are often coloured by no more than the water.

The blobs of dye (2) were applied and positioned with a wooden stick (4). The deeper the stick is dipped, the bigger the blob.

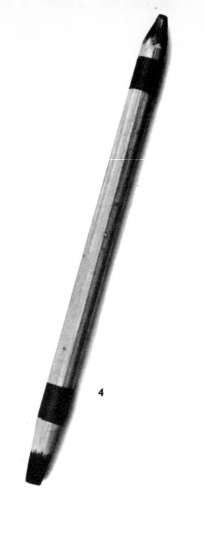

3   4   5 B 12

Circles dabbed on to the material (3) with the thick and thin ends of a sharpened stick (4), in a careful alternation of groups of large and small blobs.

Two-handed diagonal patterning by simultaneous use of two sticks (5).

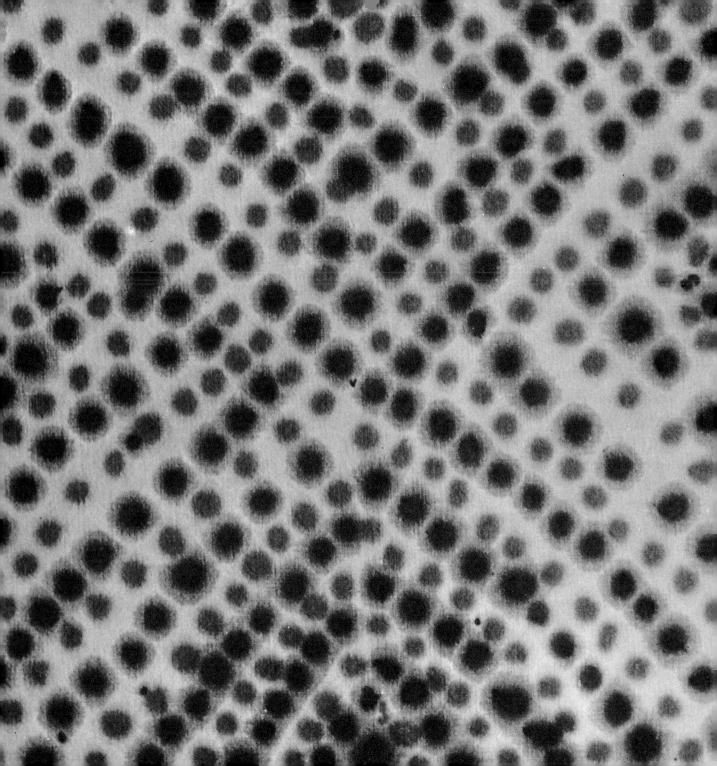

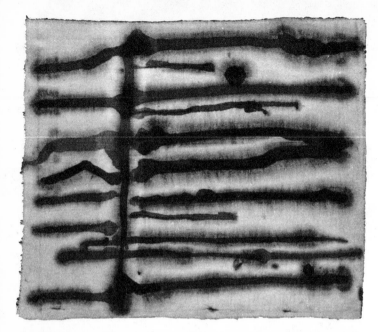

6 B 10

7 B 10

On horizontal fabric a drop of dye will form a circle. If the frame holding the stretched material is tilted, the drop runs down the slope of the frame leaving a trail of dye. The way in which the trail runs depends on the direction of tilt. In 6 the trails are arranged to run at right-angles to the vertical axis, and the almost parallel trails vary in width. The faster the dye flows over the fabric, the less it can spread. The thinner lines were obtained by holding the frame at a steeper angle.

The V-shaped patterning in 7 contains trails running from and into the central axis. Bright and dark lines of dye are made to criss-cross. Dressed cloth was used for 6-8.

8 B 10

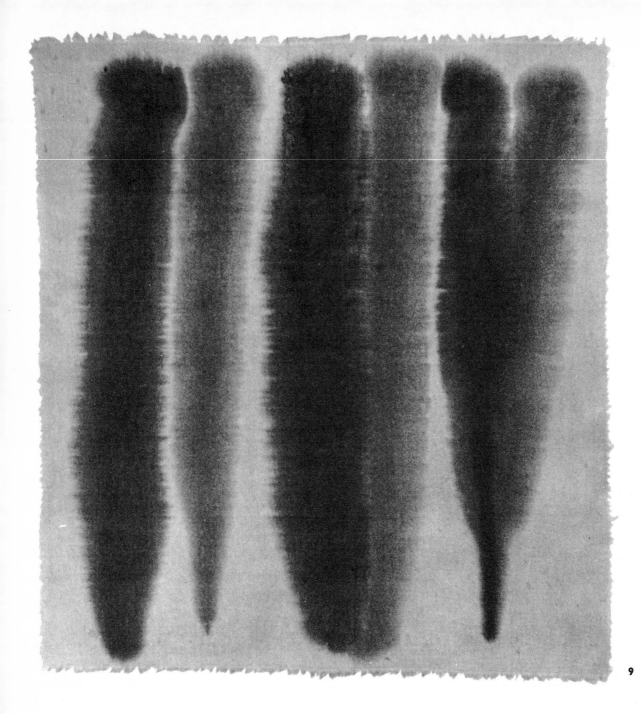

9

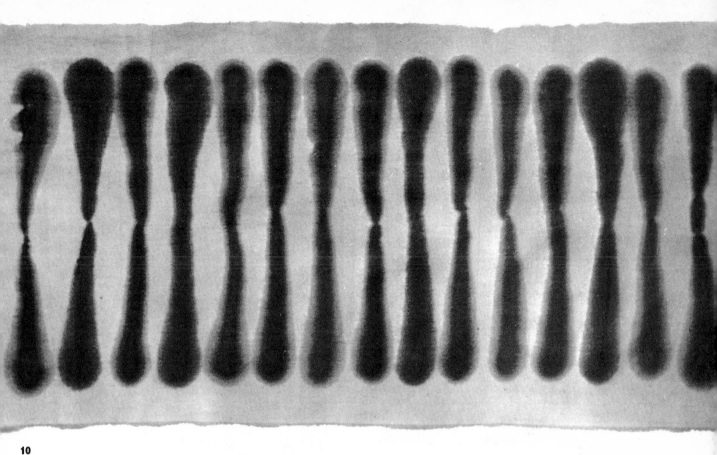

10

The trail formed by running dye on dressed fabric is narrower than that made on fabric that has been washed and is therefore more absorbent. In 9 the angle of tilt of the frame forces the dye into a broader and shorter track which ends in a narrow 'tail'.

The track can also be narrowed by drawing the dye-brush across a horizontal piece of material. Where the brush first touches the cloth, the circular spread of dye is clear. The brush stroke then carries the dye in a narrowing line until it meets the apex of the opposite track (10).

Plate I ▶

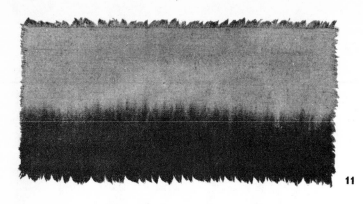

11

12

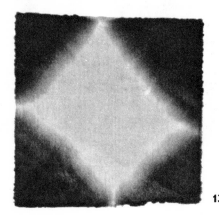

13

14

When one edge of a strip of cloth is held in a solution of dye, the dye rises up the fabric above the level of the fluid and forms zones of different intensity of colour. The borderline of colour is not straight but runs in a finely serrated, uneven line of dye.

11—Dyeing from one side; 14—Dyeing round the edges; 12—Diagonal dyeing; 13—Dyeing at corners.

If a piece of fabric is folded and dipped at the fold into a solution of dye, a dyed strip of double width appears when the piece is flattened out again, both sides showing the typical serrated borderline of dye (15). Before this 'fold and dip' process the fabric can be doubled over at varying intervals and then folded.

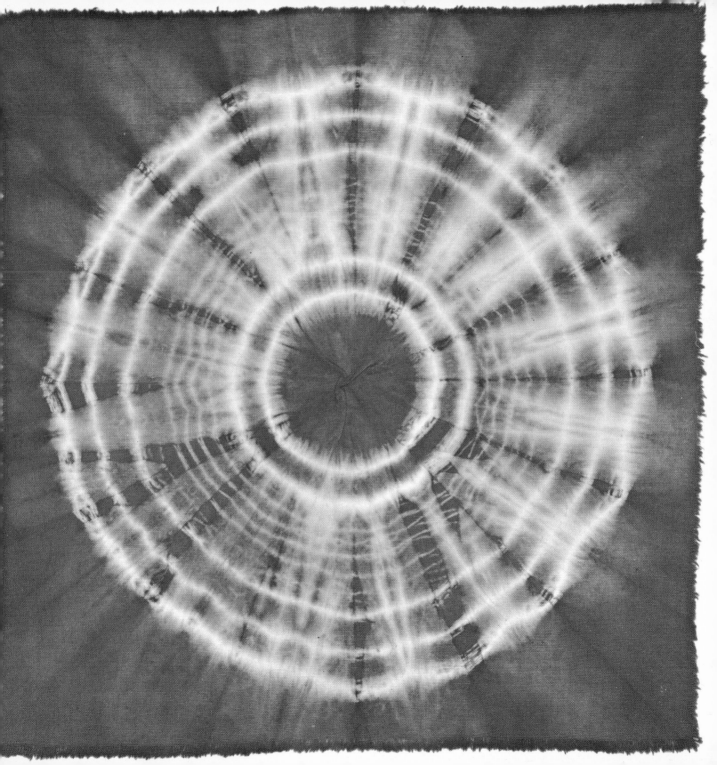

15

16

17

The linen strips illustrated in 16 and 17 have been doubled over four times before dyeing their rectangular and diagonal axes. The lines of dye are repeated fourfold, except that the width of the pattern is progressively reduced as the inner layers of cloth absorb less dye than the outer layers. This sets a limit to the number of times a pattern can be duplicated. Note that simple folds always produce the basic outline of a rectangle.

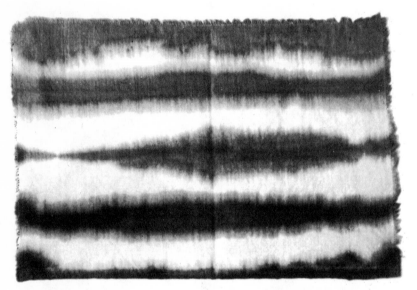

18 B 12

19 B 12

18—The cloth has been folded once down the vertical axis and then in a zig-zag. The long sides of the folded material were dipped in two solutions of dye; when unfolded, the result is alternate light and dark stripes.

19—An example of diagonal zig-zag folding.

20—Before dipping, the material was folded lengthwise and diagonally. The resulting quadrilateral was first folded along one of the diagonals and dipped in light dye, then folded along the other diagonal and dyed dark. When unfolded the material has a pattern consisting of a bright-coloured square standing on a point, overlaid with a darker diagonal cross.

20 B 12

Fold dyeing is easier to execute with large pieces of material than with small. In order not to smudge the patterns when refolding, it is advisable to dry the cloth after each dip.

21—Section of a long strip (10″×1′8″) with patterns duplicated in mirror-image.

21

22 B 12

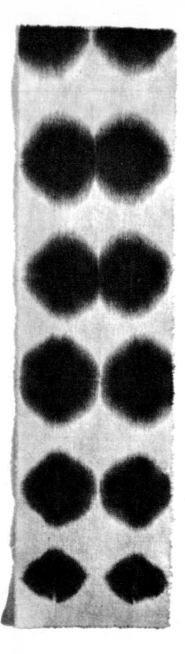

23 J 12

If an oblong strip of cloth is folded in the right-angle and diagonal method shown in 20, the result is a series of right-angled isosceles triangles. The patterns arising from dyeing the corners of these triangles can be seen from illustrations on these pages. The finished patterns which correspond to the folded pieces of cloth are: 24 and 27; 25 and 28. 30 results from a combination of 26 and 27.

When the corner is dipped the dye spreads out evenly through the fabric, except that in the crease of the fold it penetrates slightly further, so that when the fabric is unfolded, the pattern emerges not in circular but in rhomboidal shapes. The strip shown in 22 has been doubled over six times, then folded into a triangle and dyed. In 23 the double row of blobs was produced by the same method, though preceded by a longitudinal fold. Many patterns can be produced from a few combinations of folds.

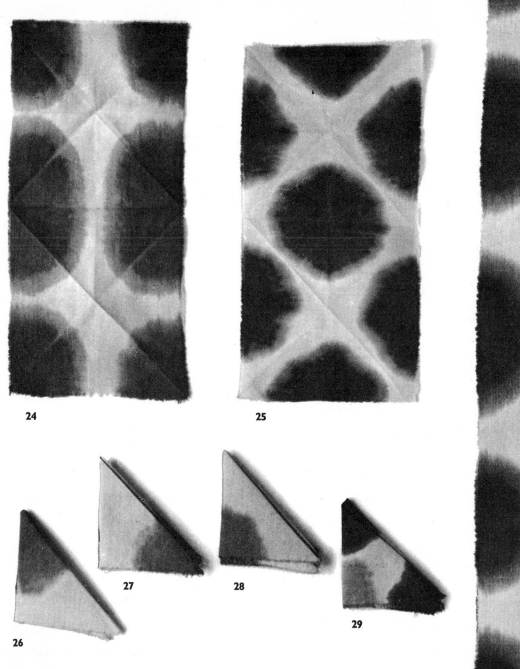
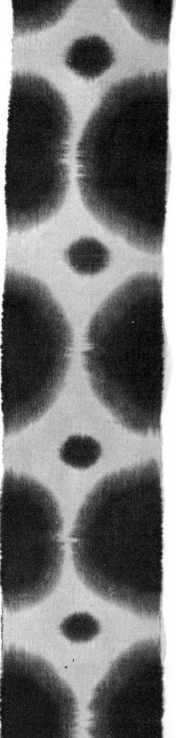

24

25

26

27

28

29

30

31 B 12 32 B 12

The piece of cloth shown in 31 is an example of a triangular fold where all three corners have been dipped.

In 32 the triangle of material was folded again. If the corners are dipped fairly deeply into the dye-bath, so that only relatively little of the basic colour of the fabric is left showing, the undyed portion of the fabric assumes the aspect of a light pattern on a dark ground (31 and 32).

In 33 the cloth has been folded lengthwise and crosswise into a square, then once more lengthwise and crosswise and once diagonally. The three corners of the resulting triangle were then dipped, at varying depths, into red, yellow and blue dyes. This method, using the same sequence as that employed in 31, produces a different, symmetrical pattern.

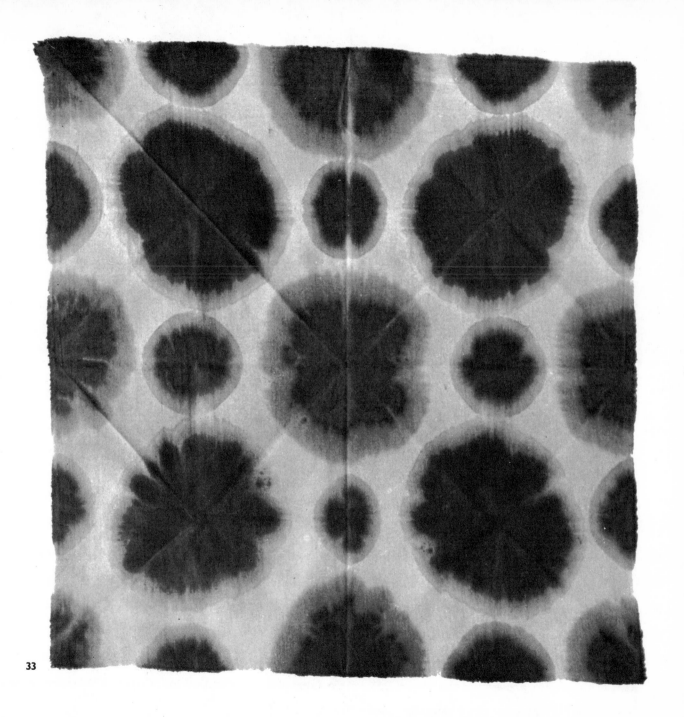

33

34 B 12

35 B 12

Line patterns and blob patterns can be used together.

In 34 the corners of the cloth were folded into the middle—in the same way that paper is folded to make an envelope—and the square folded again into a triangle. The apex and the side opposite were dipped in dye. A triangular fold is also the basis of the pattern in 35. First, two corners were dyed; the triangle was then folded across the middle, parallel to the base, and this fold dyed.

If the folded cloth is pressed firmly between finger and thumb during dying (38), the absorption of dye at these points is reduced. The pressure of the fingers 'masks' the fabric (36). The undyed inner circle of 37 was made by 'pressure-masking' the apex of a triangular piece of folded cloth (39).

24

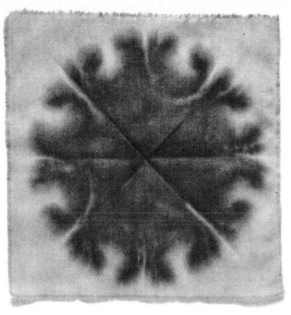

36

37

38

39

40   41

Concentric patterns can also be achieved if the square of cloth is folded, not into a triangle, but in thick folds radiating from the centre. The tighter and closer together they are, the more nearly circular will be the pattern. 40 and 41—The central circle is first masked by finger pressure and then dipped in a second dye of different colour.

42 shows a multiple design composed by juxtaposition of positive and negative circular patterns. The 'positive' circles are obtained by dipping the apex of the fold into the dye, the 'negative' ones by dipping the base of the fold and masking the apex. This piece of co-operative work was done by 13-year-old girls. Even though the same methods were used, there are obvious variations in the results, showing how individual expression can be achieved even with this simple folding technique. Group work can of course be extended to other dyeing methods.

G 13

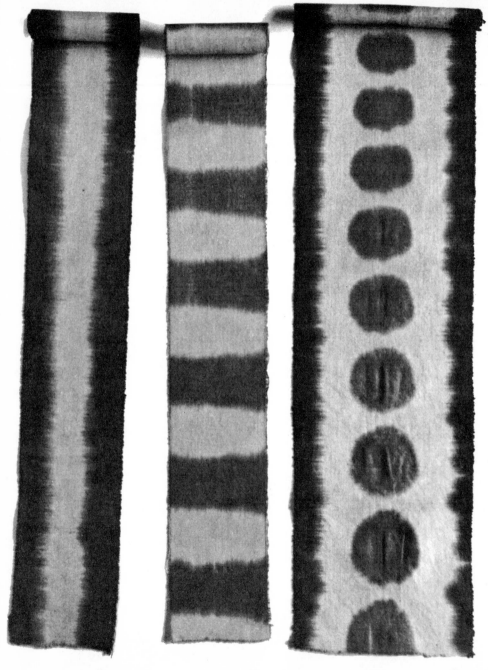

43—A long strip of cloth is rolled up and each end dipped in dye.

44—If the roll is dipped in dye along its axis to a depth of half its diameter, the result when unrolled is a series of stripes. They grow narrower and closer together towards the centre of the roll, which limits the useful length of a roll dyed in this way.

The same limitation naturally applies to the type of roll with circles in 45. Here, after dyeing each end of the rolled-up strip, it is bent double in the middle and only the point of the fold is dipped.

46—A rolled-up piece of cloth is twisted tight and dipped in a solution of pale dye. It is then dried, twisted again and partly dyed with a darker colour.

43   44   45

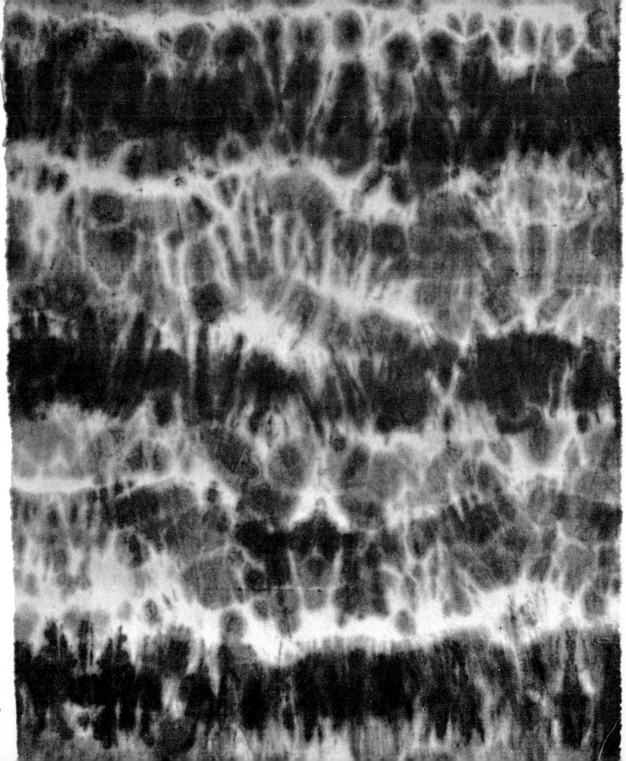

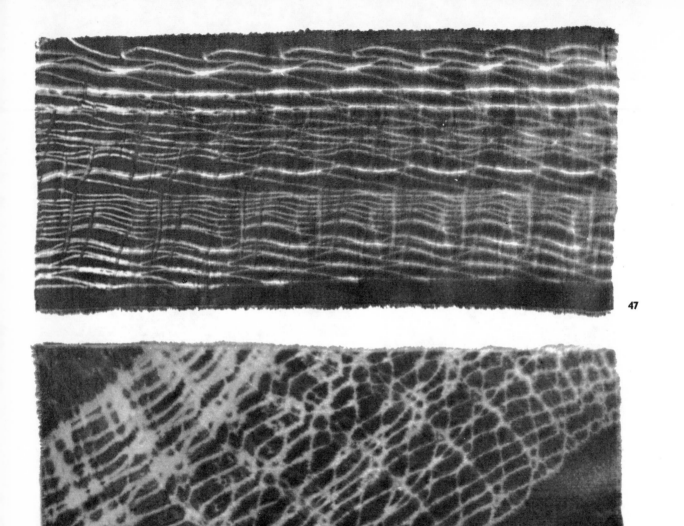

47

48 B 12

A roll of fabric is bound with string in a spiral for almost the whole of its length (49) and is then completely dipped in the dye-bath. The pressure of the binding protects the material beneath from the action of the dye. When the binding is untied the area that it has masked shows up as a pale web of lines against the dyed cloth.

49

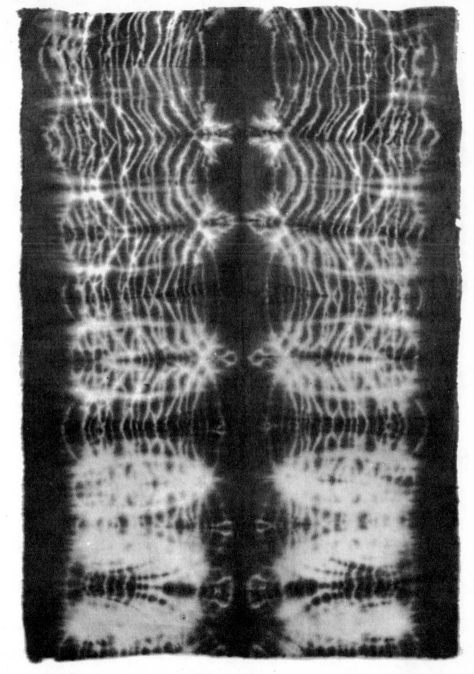

47—A roll of cloth that has been masked by binding along the direction of the thread.

48—A roll masked by binding diagonally to the direction of the thread.

50—Double masking with a binder, achieved by folding the cloth down the middle.

50 B 12

Plate II

This spider-like pattern is produced by bringing all four corners of the cloth into the middle, folding the material lengthwise and crosswise, then rolling it up, binding and dyeing it (51).

The tighter the binding, the clearer are the masked areas. To pull the string as tight as possible, one end should be knotted round the roll of cloth and the other end held firm, e.g. by standing on it. Then it can be wound round the roll of material under constant tension.

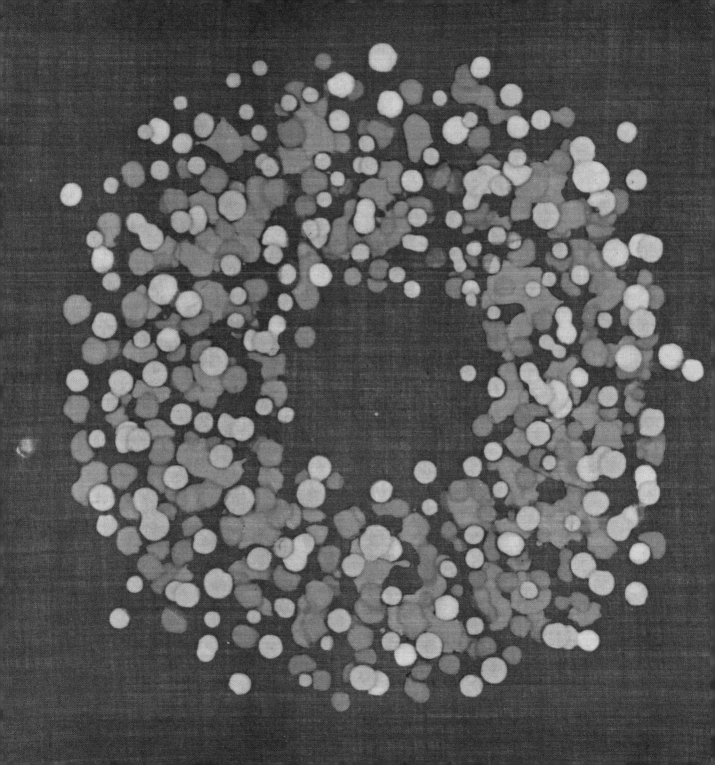

52

53

The method of masking by binding limits the size of cloth that can be used. Thick rolls cannot be dyed all through and the masking becomes blurred on the inner folds of the roll. This can be avoided by winding the roll round a central rod, e.g. a cylindrical piece of glass (52). A strip of plastic was used instead of string. After the first winding, the roll with its glass cylinder was dipped into a light-coloured dye. Further windings were then made over the first and the roll dipped again into a dye-bath of darker colour.

53—In this example the cloth was wrapped round a rubber ball.

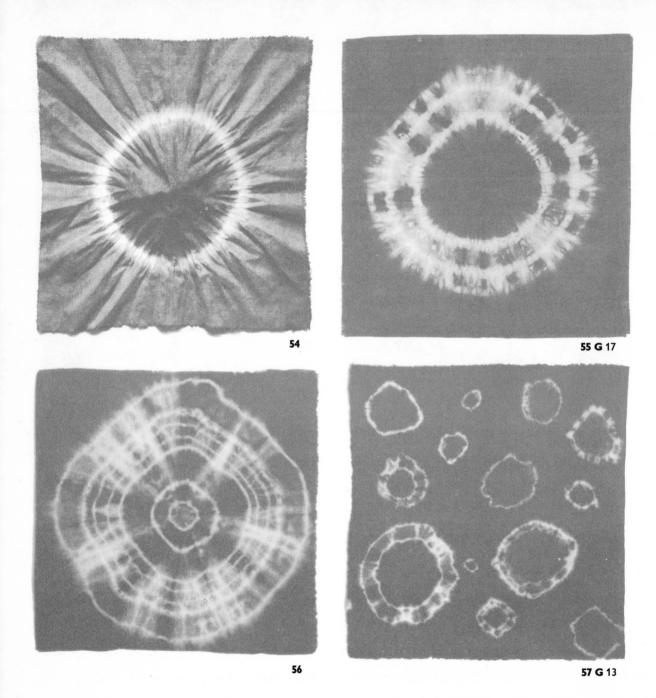

54

55 G 17

56

57 G 13

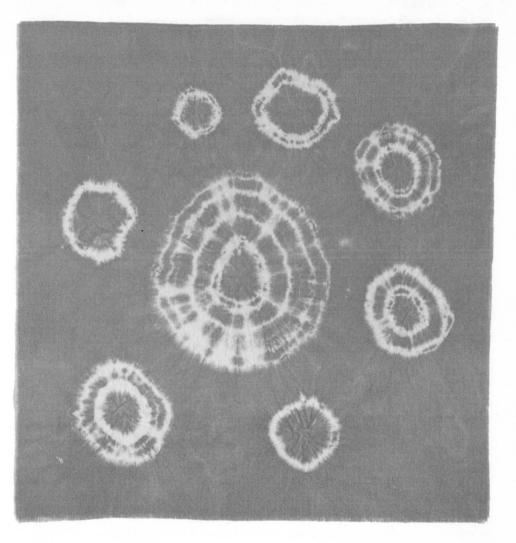

58

60—A piece of material is picked up in the middle, doubled over in thick radial folds, bound and dyed.

Masking concentric circles: single (54); triple (55); multiple (56). The material can be bound at several points to produce a 'scatter' effect (57 and 58).

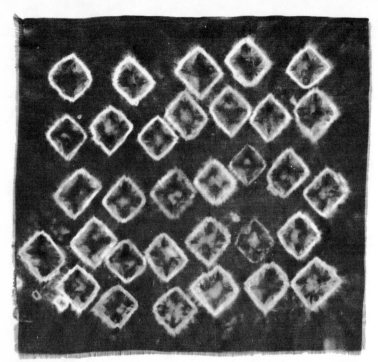

59

60

If the radial folds are laid irregularly, patterns of the kind of
those shown in 56 and 61 are the result. 61 is a section of a radially
folded piece of cloth a square yard in size.

A few folds, each with a minimum of binding, produce square or
nearly square patterns (59). The repeated pattern is given a sense
of rhythmic movement by slight variations in the shape of each
motif and the distances between them.

36

61 B 12

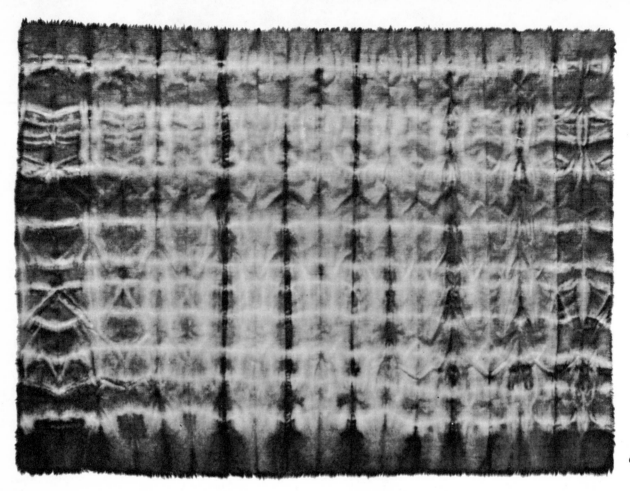

62

62—This piece of cloth was folded into accordion pleats and bound with several pieces of string; it was then dyed, first in brown and then for a short while in blue. By this means the blue dye was confined to the outer layers of the material.

The same sequence was used with the radially folded material shown in Plate I (opp. p. 16).

63—The middle section of an oblong piece of cloth was gathered into zig-zag folds, the remaining sections in folds radiating outwards from the centre. The whole was then bound and dyed.

Masking the cloth by binding is a fascinating technique which appeals to all ages. The roll of material has a plastic quality and the process of binding gives a marked tactile pleasure. When the roll is untied the unpromising-looking bundle of material unfolds to reveal a richly-patterned cloth.

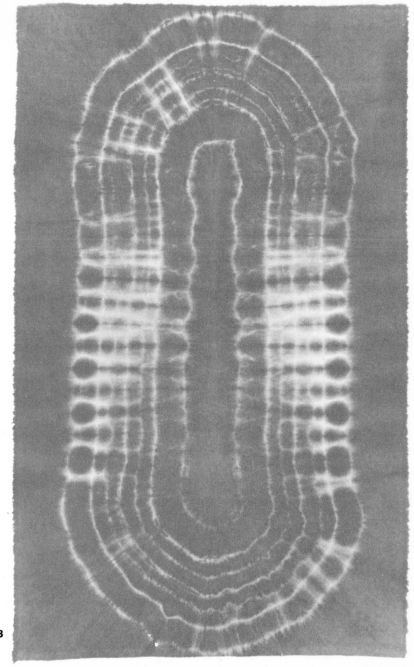

63

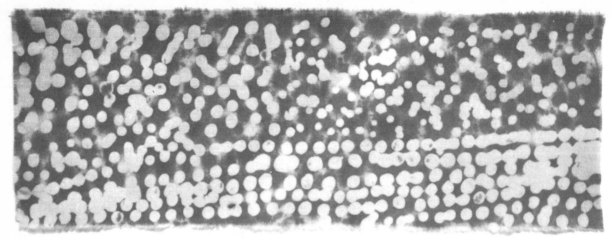

When a candle burns, a reservoir of liquid wax forms round the wick. It is held in a saucer-shaped depression by the cooler, unmelted rim of the candle. If the candle is tipped, the flame makes the upper side of the rim melt whilst the lower rim gradually lengthens. A considerable quantity of wax can collect in the space round the wick, which can easily slop over the edge and should be poured away before using the candle for dropping wax on to cloth.

The heated wax runs down the spatulate lower rim of the candle, drips on to the cloth and penetrates it. If it has to fall too far before reaching the cloth, the cooling wax falls in blobs that have insufficient adhesion to stick to the cloth, whereas in the dye-bath the wax will only mask the material if it actually penetrates the weave. For this reason the lower rim of the candle should be frequently broken off or the candle turned during the action of dropping wax. Household candles made of mineral-base wax (paraffin wax) and beeswax candles are equally suitable. After dyeing, drops of paraffin wax can largely be removed by cracking or rubbing, even without dipping them into very hot water, which melts all traces of wax out of the cloth.

64—Drops of wax were first strewn at random on the fabric and then in more ordered rows. Blue dye was then stippled on. The character of the pattern is achieved by the contrast between the sharply delineated waxed areas and the intermingling blobs of dye.

65—Patterning by dense layering with drops of candlewax. To prevent drops melting into each other they are first spread at fairly wide intervals and the gaps filled in when the first series of drops have cooled and hardened.

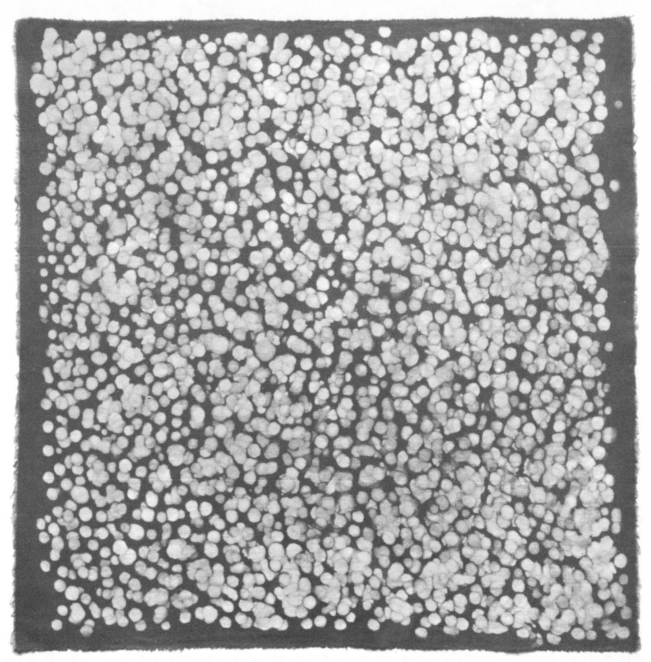

65

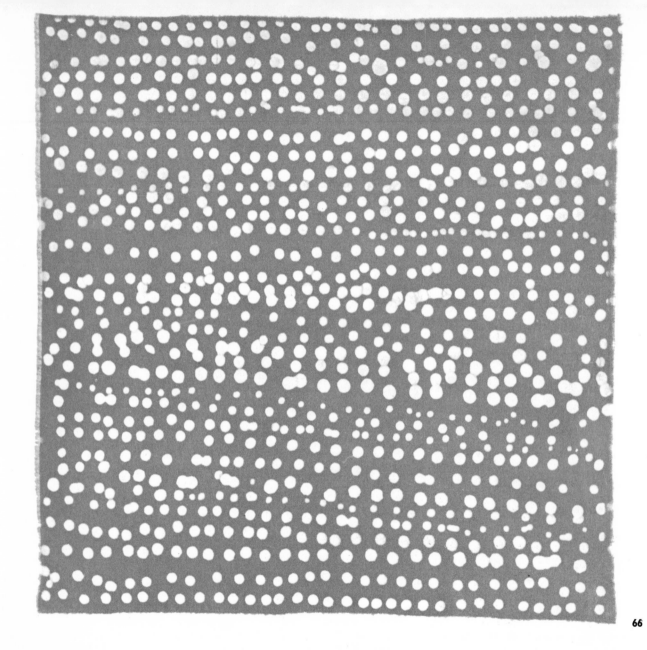

66—Rows of bright spots stand out against a red background. Changes in pattern and the size of the blobs are due to variations in the way the wax runs off the candle. The flowing or halting character of the rows is caused by the varying speed at which the wax falls.

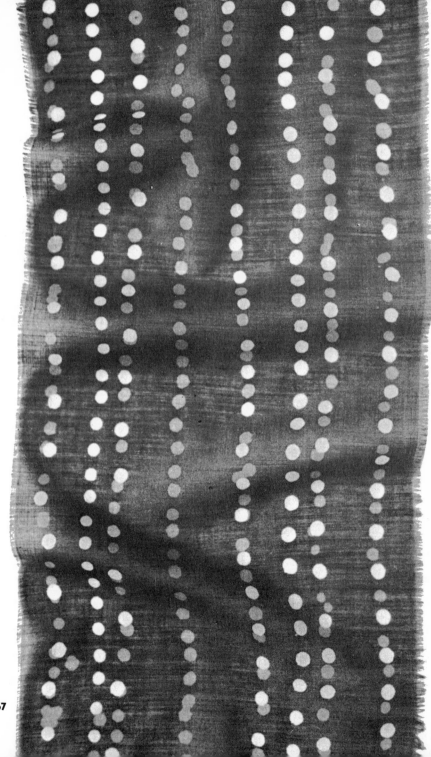

67—Wax dropped in longitudinal rows on to a scarf, masking the white fabric when it is dipped in yellow dye. A second set of drops then masks the yellow when the material is dipped again in a blue dye. This produces a pattern of white and yellow dots on bluish-green fabric. The design shown in Plate II (opp. p. 32) is produced by the same technique, except that in this case the first series of wax drops masks yellow material which is dyed red. When the red dye is dry, a further pattern of wax is applied; the cloth is dipped for a second time in a blue dye-bath and all the wax is then removed.

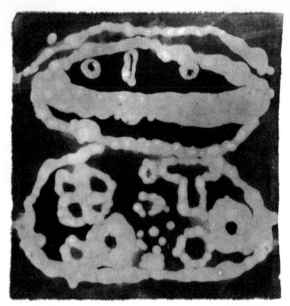

68 G 10

69 B 11

68—Here wax drops are applied so close together that they form rings, whilst remaining recognisable as a series of drops. Dye is poured on the spaces between the rings, producing the immediate result of a pattern of alternating concentric circles.

69—This design is based on wide, thick lines of candlewax laid over the material. Whereas in 68 the dye could seep out at points where the line of drops was interrupted, in this example the drops are fused into unbroken lines. The mouth was broadened by the vigorous application of several lines laid side by side. The areas within the lines were freely coloured with blue, red and yellow, the various dyes running into each other. This effect can only be achieved by direct application of dye.

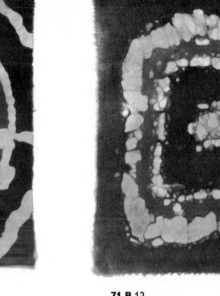

70 B 12   **71 B** 12

70—The cross placed across circles creates a relationship between the pattern and the shape of the fabric. The lines of wax have been laid thick and firm, whereas in 71 they are partly broken. The dye is dabbed on after completely soaking the fabric in water, allowing the dye to spread evenly, without forming lines or ridges of varying tone.

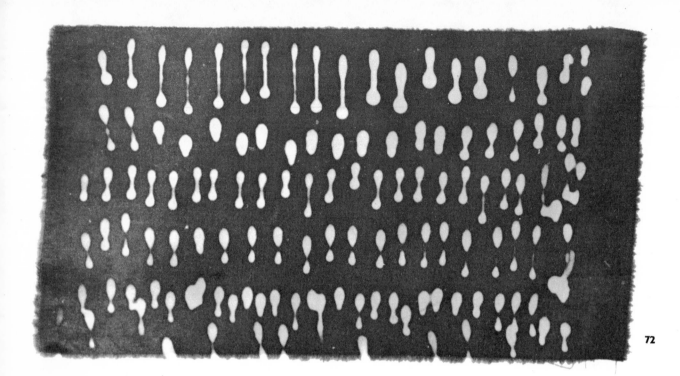

72

Candlewax has been dropped on to a linen surface which is held at a different angle after each row. When the angle is only a slight one the natural circular shape of the drops of wax lengthens to an oval (72, second row). If the angle of the cloth is steeper the wax runs down the material in a thin track, then widens out into a pear-shaped blob as it cools. These variations and the different shapes formed can be seen in 72.

Plate III (opp. p. 48)—Part of the material is shielded by trails of wax from the first dip in ochre dye. The masking is removed and another partial application of wax made to the white and ochre striped fabric. After the second dip in blue dye, the unwaxed areas emerge coloured blue and green.

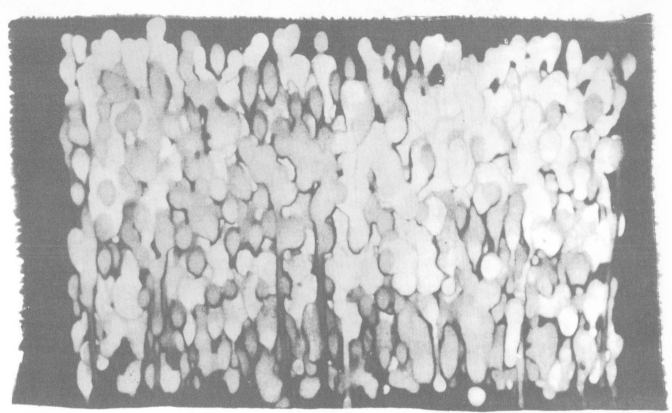

73 G 13

73—On this piece of cloth, wax has been thickly applied in several layers. Fresh wax tends to run round and past the cooled wax, producing a medley of pale and darker, partially masked areas. The dense, plastic method of application results in a free and more loosely-textured pattern in contrast to the more strictly linear pattern obtainable when using single drops of wax.

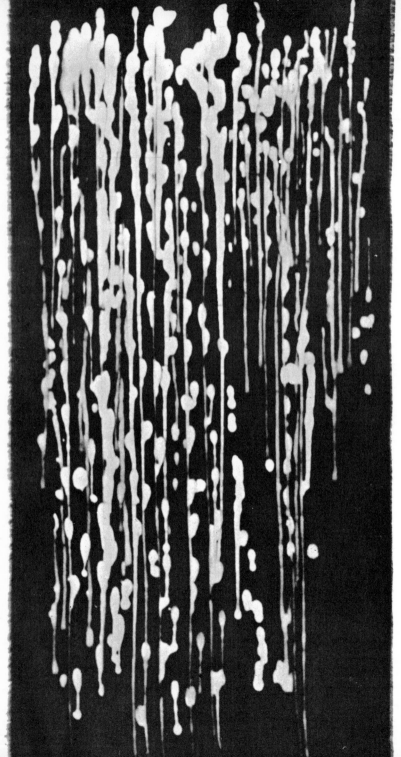

Plate III ▶

74—This effect is achieved by following the descending trails of wax with the candle and placing a close succession of drops one below the other, producing long lines broken by blobs.

Some of the lines are considerably longer and not interrupted by blobs: for these, the candle is held very close to the material to allow an unbroken trail of wax to flow down the fabric.

75—A pattern made up of lines of wax radiating from the centre. The candle is always held at the same point and the fabric rotated and tilted.

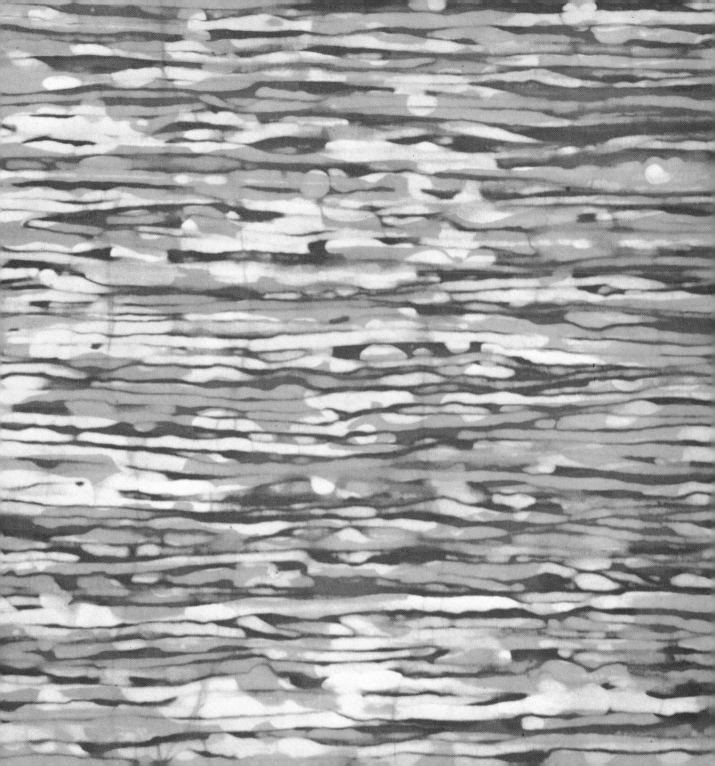

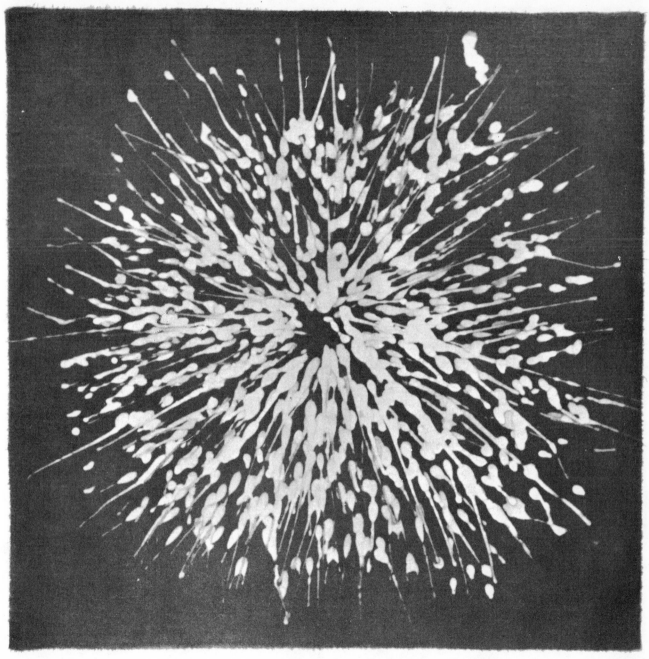

75

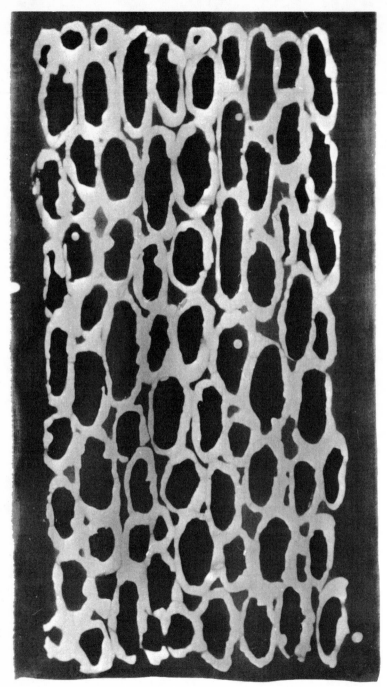

The shallower the angle of tilt of the linen fabric, the slower the drops of wax will run down it. The material should be tilted just enough to permit an easy flow without affecting the direction of flow. Under these conditions the line of wax can easily be made to change direction if the candle is held close to the fabric and a continuous flow of wax maintained.

The comparative ease, flexibility and scope of this technique make it one of the most rewarding forms of creative play with fabric and dye.

76

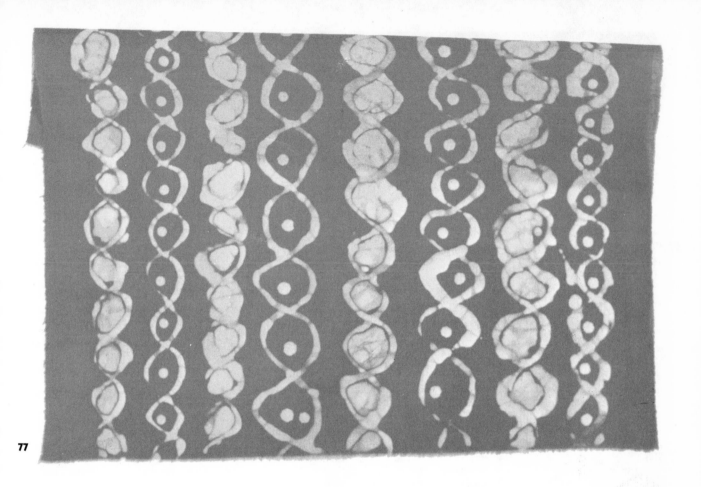

77

76—The wax is laid in wavy, criss-cross lines. The areas within the lines are decorated with pinpoint and flattened wax blobs.

77—Before the fabric was released from its frame, random 'cells' of the pattern were dyed blue, after which the whole piece of cloth was dipped in a red dye-bath. The darker colour should be applied first.

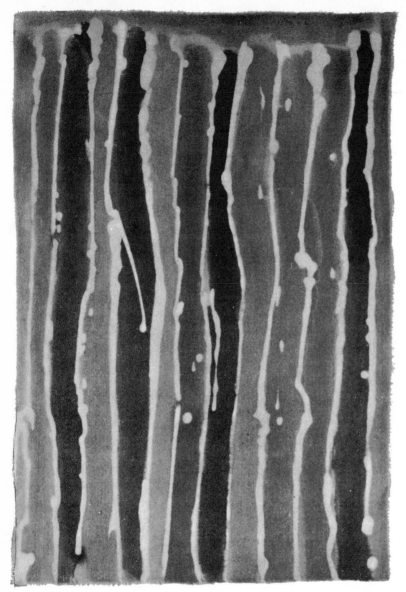

78

The line of wax becomes more controllable when the candle is held at right-angles to it and the wax flows down from the side.

78—The coloured stripes are formed by pouring dye down the channels formed by lines of wax.

79—The candle can also be held in such a way that it seems to push the line of wax in front of it. Dye is poured into the squares formed by the wax trails, spreads out to the edges and penetrates into neighbouring squares where there are breaks in the wax. Much of the attraction of this type of pattern lies in the freedom and slight irregularity of the lines of candle-wax.

A metal band is fastened round a nightlight, so that when it is lit a reservoir of liquid stearin (paraffin wax) is retained around the wick. A pointed wooden tool (83) is used to dip into the liquid wax and convey it to the fabric. When doing so the tip of the tool should be held momentarily in the flame; this warms it sufficiently to prevent the wax from cooling too quickly before it is applied to the cloth. The size of the blob of wax depends on how deep the tool is dipped. Patterning with a tool is precise, enabling the exact spot to be selected for the wax blob, which can then be extended into a shape like a comma by drawing out the wax in one direction. These can be placed singly or in groups.

80—Groups of 'tadpoles' made into a pattern of conventionalised stars.

82—A circular pattern made by turning the fabric as the extended blobs of wax are applied.

80

81

82

83

84

85

These rag dolls are dressed in fabrics decorated by wax lines and printing (Plate IV, opp. p. 64), by cracked wax (84) and by masking with the tjanting method (85) and with drops of candlewax (86).

56

86

Fabric can be masked with mineral wax or with beeswax. Mineral wax can be bought in the shops under the name of paraffin wax. When certain substances are added to it to ensure even burning, it is known as stearin, the basic material used to make candles.

Beeswax is the substance with which bees build honeycombs. To obtain beeswax, a honeycomb should be melted in hot water. When the water has cooled the pure wax can be scooped off the surface, where it will have collected. Mineral wax melts at 176° Fahrenheit (80° Centigrade), beeswax at 140° Fahrenheit (60° Centigrade). If it is heated too much, wax may froth up and burn away. Wax that is too hot will drip off the tools for applying it to the fabric, and the lines, dots or patches may spread out in unexpected places and penetrate unnecessarily deep into the fibres of the material. When this happens they are hard to remove. Wax that is too cold adheres only slightly or not at all to the surface of the fabric, easily flakes off and does not mask the cloth sufficiently from the dye. In masking techniques, therefore, in which wax is used in fairly large quantities, it is essential to maintain the liquid wax at as even a temperature as possible.

For this reason the wax should be heated in a bath of water. The most practical means of doing this is with an ordinary glue-pot (88), obtainable from an ironmonger. It consists of two containers, a larger one of copper for the water and a smaller one, resting in it, for the wax. The water-level should be frequently checked and there should always be a supply of water on hand to top it up. The best form of heating is an electric ring, whose heat is more constant and easier to regulate than an open flame.

Beeswax is more malleable than paraffin wax. With its lower melting point it also remains liquid for longer after it has been removed from the pot, and is therefore better suited than mineral wax for masking with a 'dropper' or with a tjanting. Mineral wax, which is cheaper, should be used for covering large areas or for coarse work with a brush or a spoon. Paraffin wax can also be used for its brittleness, to make patterns from the cracks formed when patches of wax are snapped.

When the fabric has been dyed and has been left to dry, much of the wax should be rubbed off or scraped off with a blunt tool. This enables the rest of the wax to be removed quickly by further chemical or mechanical means.

The chemicals used for removing wax are benzine or benzole, both of which are inflammable. The equally effective carbon tetrachloride will certainly not catch fire, but because of its toxic vapour should only be used where there is good ventilation.

The mechanical method, dissolving the wax by heat, is simpler and safer. The fabric should be put between several layers of paper. If a hot iron is applied, the wax will be absorbed by the paper. The paper should be changed frequently, although even then isolated spots of burnt wax tend to form and are hard to remove. If large quantities of wax are ironed out, some of it penetrates the entire fabric; this leaves traces of wax which do give the dyes a soft, smooth patina but tends to stiffen the cloth.

87

The softness and flexibility of the cloth is retained if water is used to remove the wax. The cloth is placed in a tub with a generous quantity of hot water (175°-195° Fahrenheit) and stirred with a stick. The wax is released and floats to the surface, where it can be scooped off and used again. An equally thorough method is to use running hot water.

In all the examples illustrated in this book the wax was removed with hot water.

88

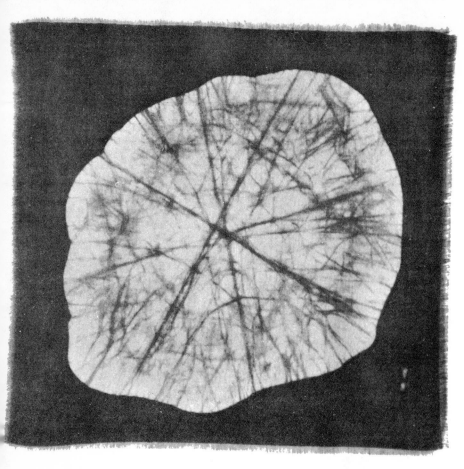

89

A large quantity of liquid paraffin wax is poured on to the fabric, it soaks through, leaving behind a patch of wax. Dipped in cold water, the wax adhering to the cloth hardens quickly and can then (as in 89) be cracked in various directions. When the material is dyed the colour penetrates the cracks and soaks into the fabric. The wax is removed, leaving a bright patch criss-crossed with a fine pattern of lines.

If two pieces of cloth are laid together and stretched the wax will penetrate both layers. The insides of the two cloths stick together. When they are separated the wax is left in patches, some on one piece of cloth, some on the other. This produces an effect of partial masking with blurred outlines and random patterning.

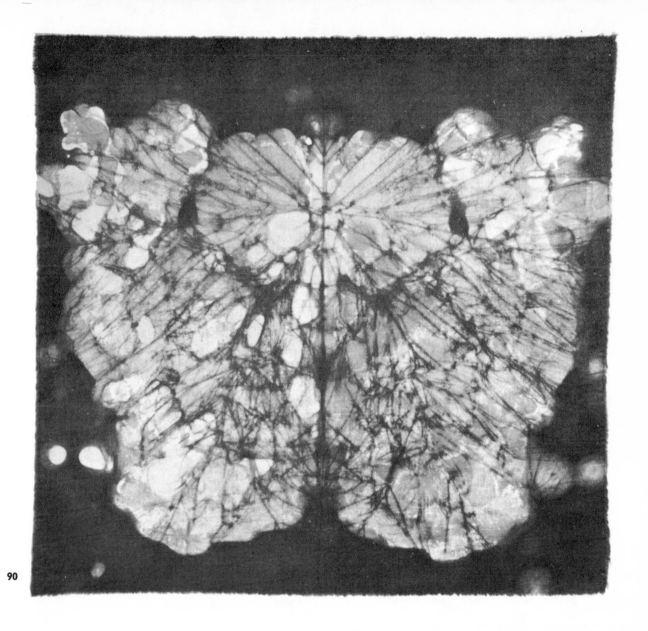

90—The fabric was folded lengthwise and wax poured on it. When the wax had hardened it was broken apart, opened out and dyed. The symmetry of the masked pattern has been modified and softened by the irregular pattern of cracks and unmasked areas.

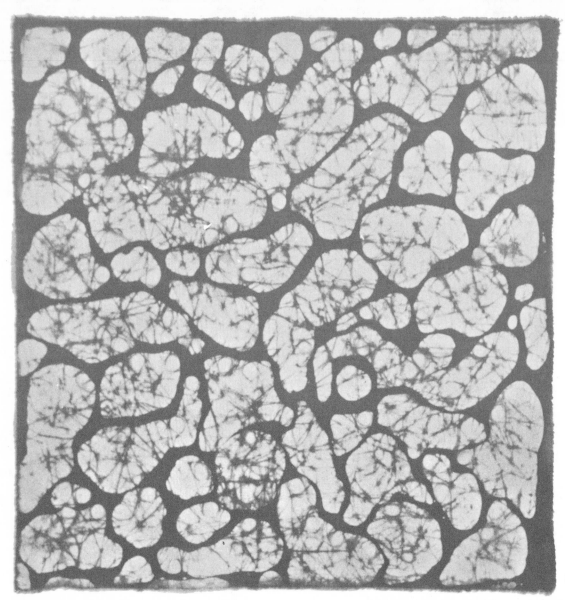

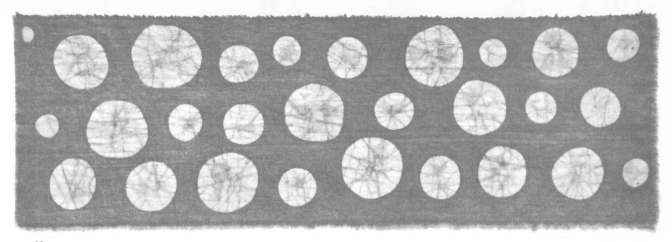

92

91—Wax is poured on to the fabric with a spoon. The different sizes and shapes of the waxed patterns result from varying the amount of wax applied to each spot. To make the cracks in the wax the whole piece of cloth (approx. 2′ × 2′) was dipped in cold water and firmly crushed into a ball. If there are not enough cracks or they are not satisfactorily placed, the cloth can be squeezed and crushed again after the first dip and then re-dyed.

92—A more orderly form of patterning is to drop a limited quantity of liquid wax on to one spot, where it will spread out into a roughly circular shape.

These spots cannot exceed a certain size, as the wax cools rapidly at the edges in spreading out. The blobs are cracked individually.

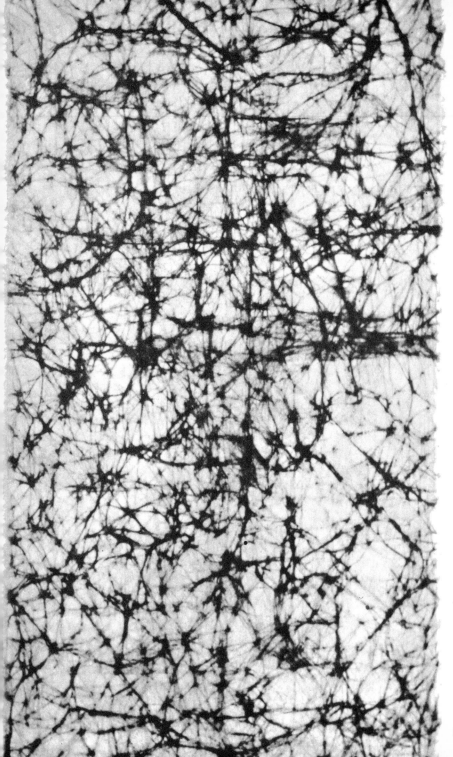

Plate IV ▶

A strip of fabric can be dipped whole in wax. This method is not particularly economical, as much more wax adheres to the cloth than is necessary for masking. Also, with large pieces of cloth, spreading out the hot waxed fabric is extremely difficult.

93—Patterns made by dye in the cracks of a strip of waxed cloth.

The wax is best applied thinly—with a broad paint brush or with a piece of folded linen—taking care that the strips of wax are applied without a break or gap between them. If it is applied unevenly, surplus wax collects at the lowest points on the underside of the material and shows up as cell-like patches in the linear pattern formed by the cracks in the wax (94).

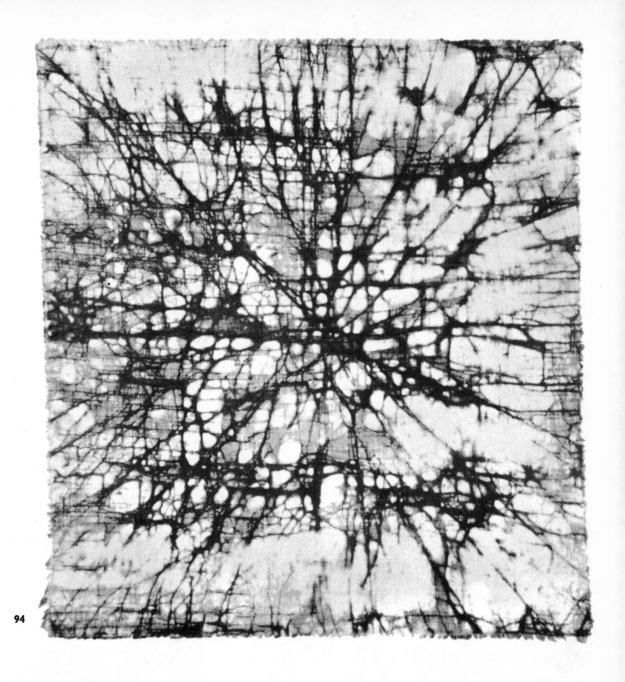

94

94—Pattern formed by radial cracks and cell-shaped patches.

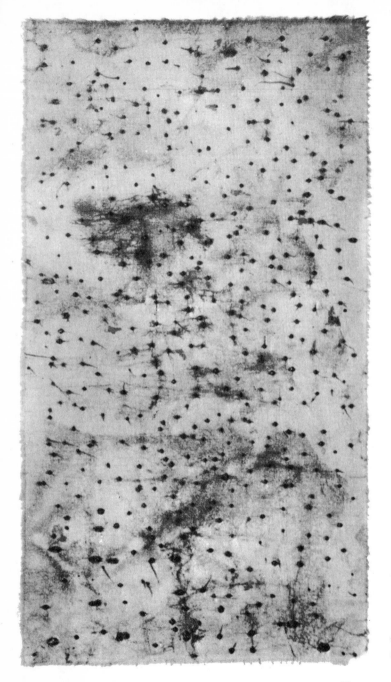

95

96

97

98

A dotted pattern can be produced by piercing the layer of wax with a nail, as in 95. The rows of dots in 96 were made with a cogwheel with pointed teeth. This method has the disadvantage of damaging the fibres of cotton and the fabric is rendered less durable.

If a piece of cloth is partly dipped in liquid wax it can be folded, in a way similar to the folding techniques mentioned in an earlier section of the book, although with the difference that it only takes on colouring in the second process of the sequence.

97—Pattern formed by a central fold.

98—Masking with a triangular fold.

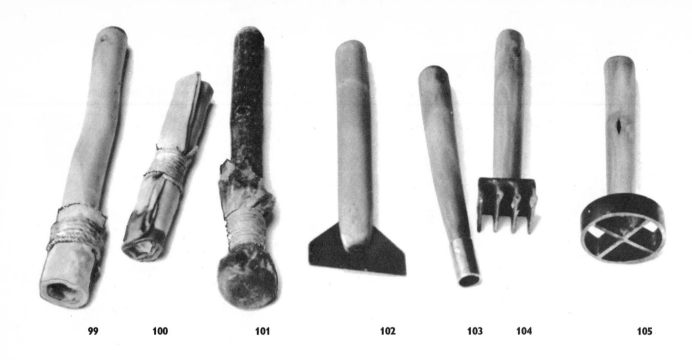

99   100   101   102   103 104   105

Another method of applying wax to fabric is with a stamp. This relies on the 'temperature gap' between the heat of the wax in the pot (up to 212° F) and the melting point of wax (between 140° and 176° according to the type-wax). A stamp can be made from material as simple as a strip of linen rolled up and tied together (see 100). If a linen roll of this type is dipped into liquid wax to a moderate depth (about $^3/_8''$ deep), it picks up enough wax to mask the circular area of fabric to which it is applied (see 132).

If a strip of linen is tied to a round stick to project beyond its end (99), it will make a ring-like impression on the fabric (108). Linen tied round a squared-off piece of wood will mask off a roughly rectangular shape (107). A stick with the end padded and covered with a piece of linen (101) will stamp circles (106), which can be slightly altered in size by varying the pressure on the stick.

Linen stamps are easy to make. The patterns which they print are irregular, because the linen remains elastic even when coated in hot wax. Making one's own tools encourages experiment and invention. The tool becomes an extension of the hand and enlarges its scope, making a unity of process and artefact.

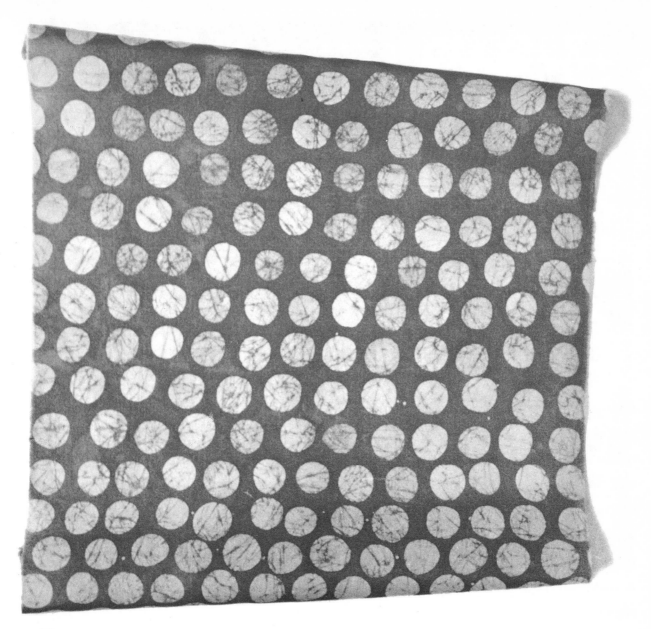

106

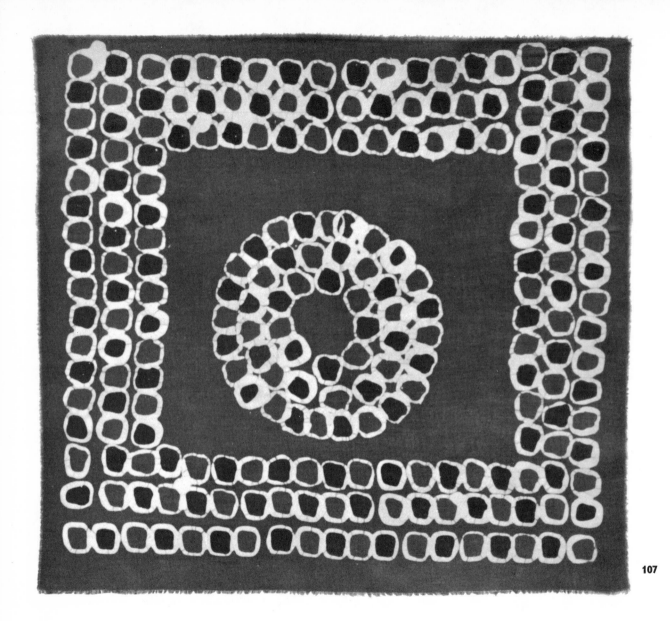

107

107—The squares were impressed with wax and filled with different colours, after which the whole piece of cloth was dipped in dye.

70

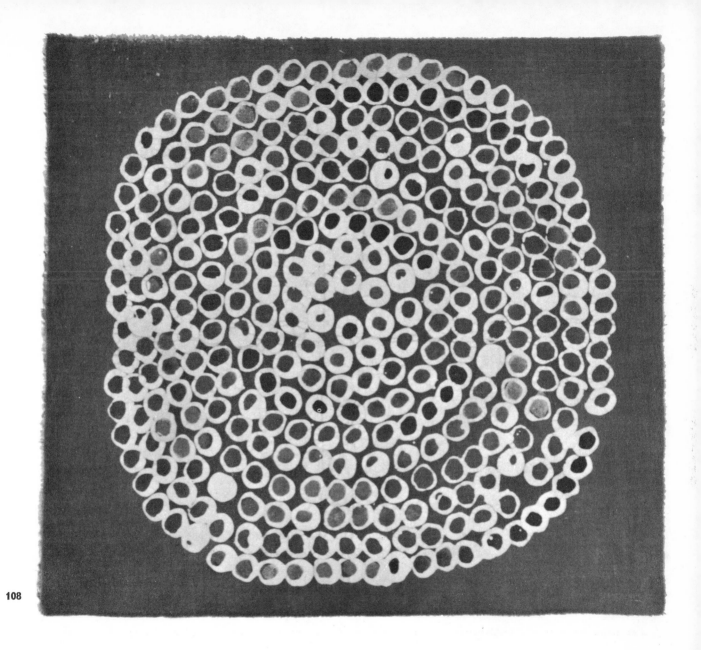

108

108—The same multiple technique as in 107. The areas within the circular stamp-marks were filled in with several colours, the whole piece then dyed.

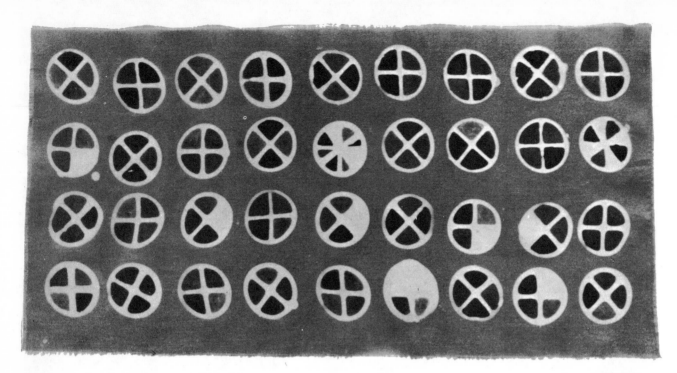

Besides flexible linen stamps one can also make more durable stamps out of metal. Copper or brass is a good conductor of heat and rapidly assumes the temperature of the heated wax. Wax will stick to the brass in a thin layer and run off when the tool is applied to fabric. Brass strip or tubing is an excellent material for making rigid stamps, because it is both fairly ductile and keeps its shape well once formed. Although it can only be used for making stamps of simple, basic pattern, these can be highly versatile in use.

102—A slot is cut in the end of a stick and a strip of brass measuring $2'' \times 1''$ and approximately $\frac{1}{16}''$ thick is inserted into the slot to form the simplest kind of stamp. An example of its use is shown in Plate V (opp. p. 80).

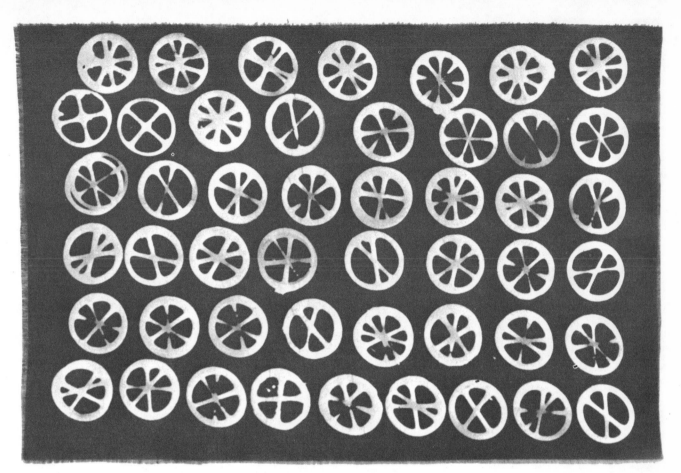

110

To make a ring-shaped stamp (103) a stick is sharpened to a point and rammed into one end of a section of brass tubing. A variation of this is made by soldering one or two cross-pieces into the tube (105). The patterns made by the 'ring and cross' stamp are given variety and vitality by the way in which the cross is turned on its axis, the varying degree of masking with individual stamps and the use of different colours in the segments of the circles (109). If the stamp is impressed more than once on the same spot variation can be introduced into the patterns made by the cross-pieces (110); more scope is given if a second stamp is used with a ring of the same diameter and a single cross-piece.

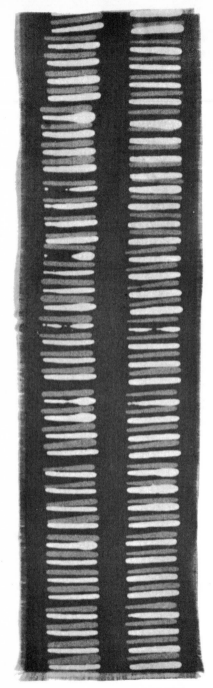

104—This stamp was made by soldering four parallel strips of brass to a base-plate. The stamp is connected to the wooden handle—as also in 105 —by a short length of tubing.

In 111 the uniformity of the elements of the pattern is varied by differences in their colour and grouping.

If the impressions of the quadruple stamp are superimposed at right-angles the result is a pattern of squares (112). Within this fairly rigid framework a free design is achieved by random colouring of the small squares. A similar effect is observable in Plate V (opp. p. 80).

111

112

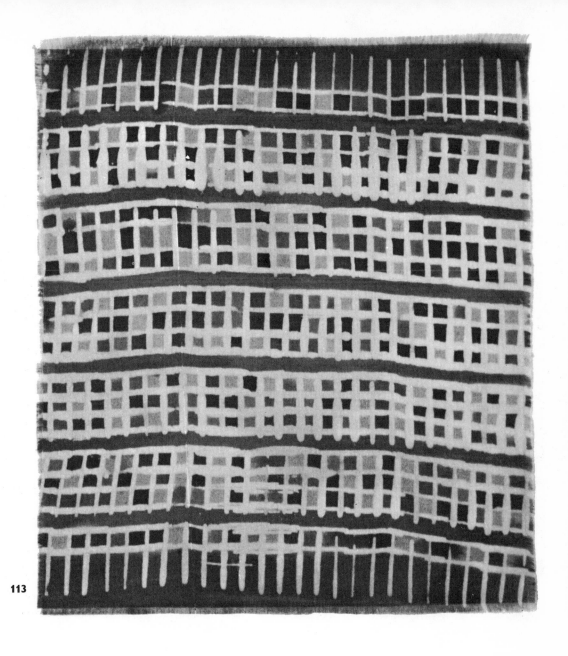

113

113—This pattern with its effect of strips of mesh is made by alternate horizontal and vertical applications of the four-line stamp. The spaces left between strips accentuate the transverse linear character of the design.

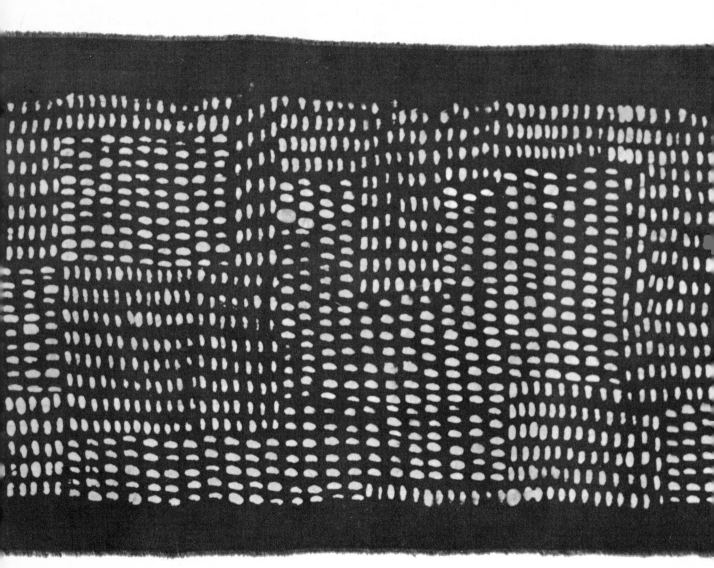

When using a flat bristle brush (118) to apply a pattern, the impression that it makes on the fabric can be altered by slightly varying the pressure on the brush. This technique has been used in 114, where rectangular groups of brush-marks are articulated into a pattern on a ground dyed dark blue.

117—This is another type of brush made of hemp bound with string. The ends are frayed to make a flattened or rounded brush, which changes shape as the pressure of the hand is increased or reduced. The marks made by this kind of brush in 115 give an easy, loosely articulated rhythmic pattern.

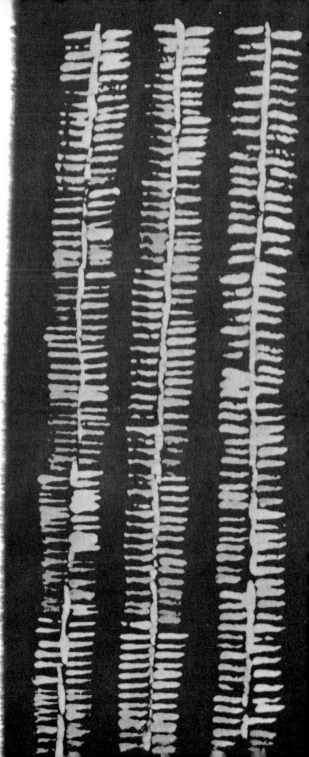

115

116

117

116—A pattern made with a hemp brush (117). The line of wax is always of equal width but varies in length according to the amount of wax on the brush and the time it takes to cool. With every new application of the brush the direction of the line is changed.

118

119

The bristle brush (118) is considerably more flexible than the hemp brush; it will be clear from the design in 119 that this method allows great freedom in making patterns of a calligraphic type.

Plate V ▶

120

121

The square and oblong patterning in 120 was produced by using two cut-down paint brushes, one broad (as in 121) and one narrow. The design made in this way can only be properly appreciated after the material has been dyed. Cracks in the wax serve to soften the contrast between the dyed and masked areas.

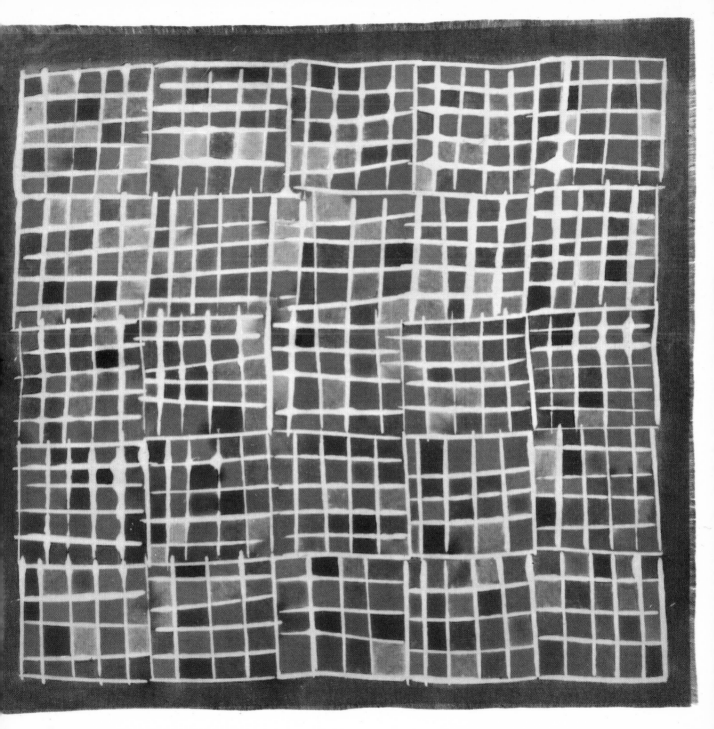

122

The robust simplicity and relative inflexibility of a broad paint-brush is exemplified in this design of squares. Each stroke is no longer than the width of the brush. In 122 the fabric was dipped in the same dye-bath each time after a few more squares had been masked. At the end of the process all the wax masking was removed together. The different colour tones result from the varying length of exposure to the dye.

123—Broad stripes of wax were applied at varying intervals; the cloth was then dyed yellow and the wax removed. Parts of the yellow and white striped fabric were again masked with stripes of wax. The second dye-bath, red this time, dyed the white areas red and the yellow areas orange. In 124 the brush strokes were applied vertically and horizontally.

125

Wax lines form a barrier to the dye in its natural tendency to spread out in a circular patch on the fabric. Wherever there is a break in the wax the dye will seep through the opening and spread out in a fan-shaped stain.

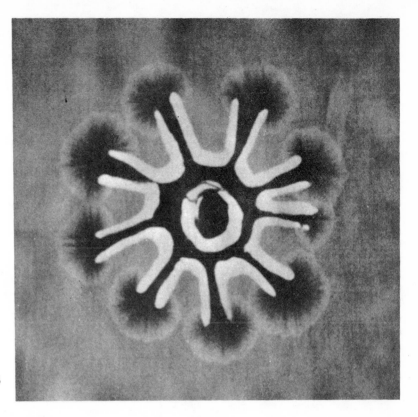

126

125 shows a pattern formed by two concentric circles of V-shaped wax lines joined at their tops by a short stroke of the brush. Dye is then poured into the space between the lines and fills it out. In 126 above, a similar pattern has been made with the spaces between the 'V's left open, so that the dye poured into the middle spreads out of the openings to form a fan-like pattern of dye at the end of each channel. The designs of this and the following two examples are based on the contrast between the confined and unconfined spread of dye.

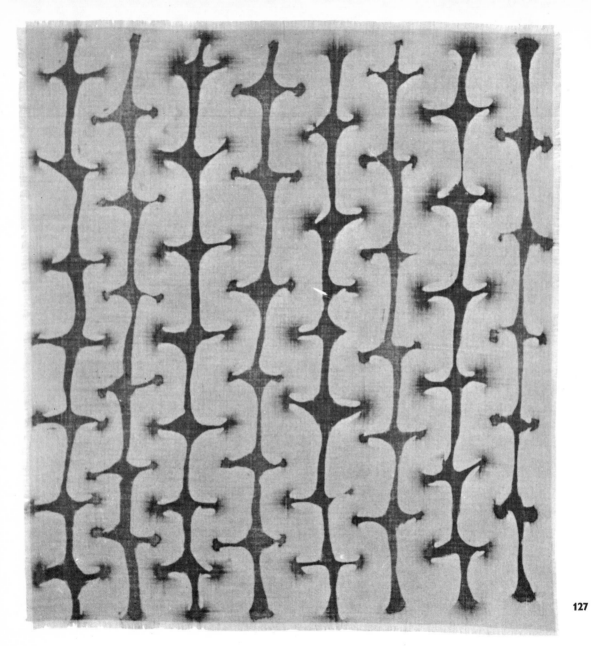

127

127—This design is made up of vertical rows of broad U-shaped figures which face each other in pairs. Dye was poured between the lines of wax and flowed out of the openings to form the characteristic patterns of free-spreading dye.

86

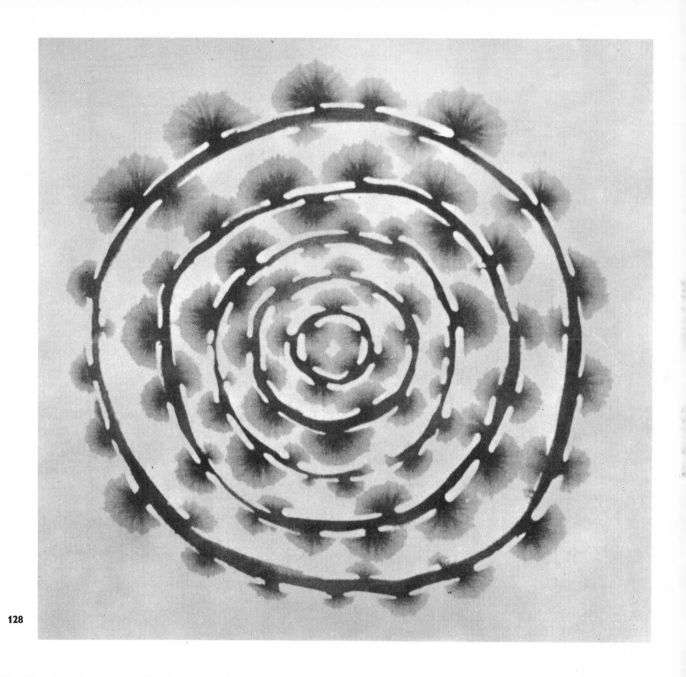

128

128—The double concentric circles of wax have been deliberately interrupted to make openings for the dye to flow out. Some of the fan-like patterns have been enlarged by pouring in extra dye near the openings.

129

129—The two basic elements of this design—the square and the triangle—were applied in wax to the fabric by the use respectively of the thin side and the thick side of a bristle brush.

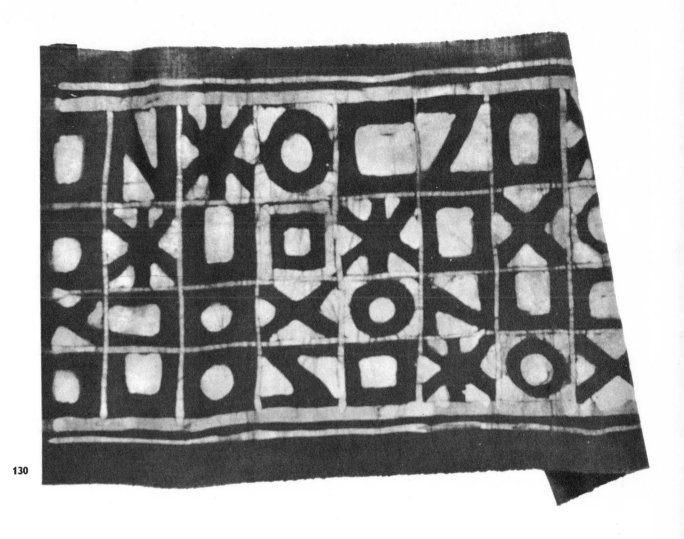

130

130—Again the framework of the design is a thin lattice of squares. Here the contrasting element is a series of geometric patterns repeated with variations.

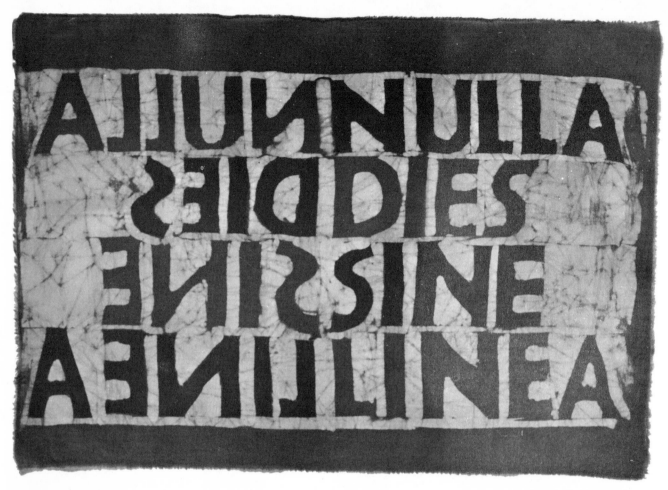

131

131—As with all the examples in the book, this pattern of lettering was produced by masking the fabric without any preliminary drawing or tracing on the fabric. The linear nature of the design is emphasised by the 'mirror image' repetition of the letters.

132

132—The squares were first outlined in wax and then filled in. The white dots were masked by using the stamp made of rolled linen (100). This combination of several methods gives greatly increased creative scope, but demands complete familiarity with the various techniques.

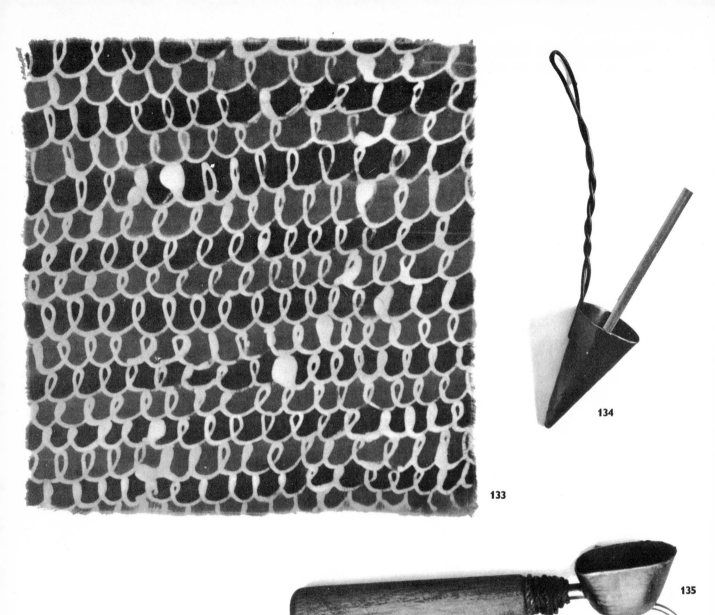

The tool illustrated in 135 is a small metal can mounted on a wooden handle; the wax drips out of the spout on to the fabric, allowing a continuous line of wax of even width to flow on to the fabric.

133—The alternate rows of dye are carefully applied between the looped lines of wax masking.

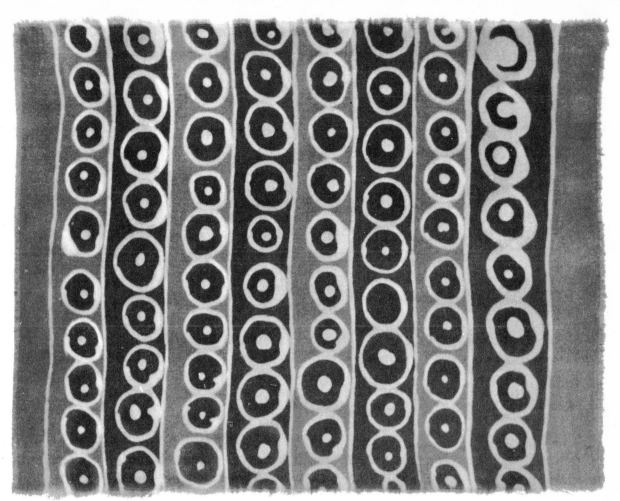

136

134—This instrument is a copper funnel with a hole in its point closed by a wooden stopper. By raising the stopper slightly the wax flows rapidly out of the funnel. The lines must therefore be drawn fast and with great sureness over the fabric (see 136).

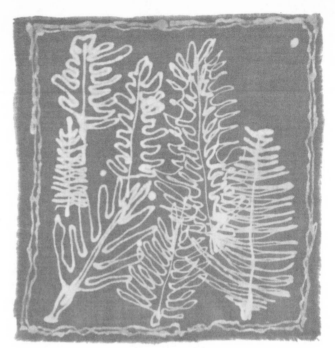

137 138

The Javanese tjanting (87) is a simple tool, in which form and function are clearly combined. The container, made of thin brass, is warmed before being dipped into the hot wax. In use the tool is held by its bamboo handle and the curved spout is drawn across the fabric very close to the surface. The front part of the bamboo handle beneath the container is intended to catch any wax which may drip over the sides. If the tool is lifted with the front end uppermost the wax cannot run out of the spout. In the case of the wax dropper illustrated in 135, the spout has to be closed by holding a rag beneath it. A rag should also be used to remove wax that runs over the sides and down the spout, which is apt to cause unintentional blobs (see 133).

An inadequate flow of wax may be due to lumps of carbonised material, thread, etc. The first step in clearing the spout is to heat it. If this has no effect it is not advisable to clean it with a wire; this can easily damage the thin cooper pipe. The best way is to blow down it.

137—A free pattern of flowing lines produced with the tjanting.

138—Plant-like forms achieved by a slight variation of the same technique.

94

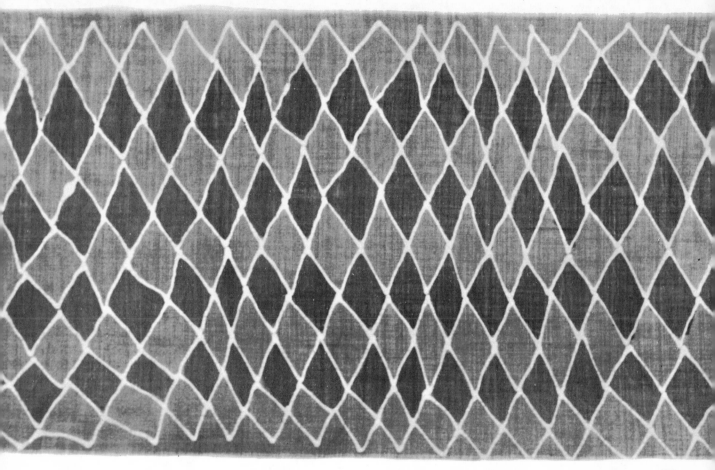

The pattern-making scope of the tjanting is very wide. The free-flowing patterns achieved in 137 and 138 are in marked contrast to the strict, austere, geometric patterning of the design shown in 139, produced by the same method.

140

The lines and patterns produced by reverse masking give an impression of a certain stiffness and lack of spontaneity compared with designs made with directly applied wax lines. The outlines of the pattern were first applied, then the rest of the masked area filled in with the brush and the wax made to crack after it had been hardened.

DATE DUE

AG 12 '72
pd

APR 11 '78

DEC 8

FEB 25 '85

JUL 2 8 '86

SEP 1 9 1996

022808

Fordham Equip. Co.

D8